HEALING
WORDS
from the
ANGELS

HEALING
WORDS
from the
ANGELS

365 Daily Messages

Doreen Virtue, Ph.D.

LIFE
Styles

HAY HOUSE, INC.

Carlsbad, California • New York City
London • Sydney • Johannesburg
Vancouver • Hong Kong • New Delhi

Published and distributed in the United States by: Hay House, Inc.: www.hayhouse. com • **Published and distributed in Australia by:** Hay House Australia Pty. Ltd.: www.hayhouse.com.au • **Published and distributed in the United Kingdom by:** Hay House UK, Ltd.: www.hayhouse.co.uk • **Published and distributed in the Republic of South Africa by:** Hay House SA (Pty), Ltd.: www.hayhouse.co.za • **Distributed in Canada by:** Raincoast: www.raincoast.com • **Published in India by:** Hay House Publishers India: www.hayhouse.co.in

Editorial supervision: Jill Kramer • *Design:* Bryn Starr Best
Illustrations: Audrey Rawlings Arena: **www.fantasyartbyaudrey.com** •
Glenda Green: **www.lovewithoutend.com** and PicturesNow.com

The material in this book was adapted from the *Messages from Your Angels Perpetual Flip Calendar,* by Doreen Virtue, Ph.D. (Hay House, 2005).

Library of Congress Control Number: 2005939099

ISBN: 978-1-4019-1196-6

13 12 11 10   5 4 3 2
1st printing, October 2007
2nd printing, August 2010

Printed in China

INTRODUCTION

The Law of Free Will says that the angels can only help you when you ask them, or give them permission to, yet many people say that they forget to ask for their angels' help. So, I've created this book to give you daily reminders to ask for your angels' assistance with anything and everything.

All the entries within come directly from the angels, so when you see the words *we* and *us*, know that the angels are personally speaking to you and are bringing you comfort, guidance, and Heavenly love. By reading their words daily, you'll be immersed in the sweet energy of their love. This will help you be more aware of your own guardian angels' messages for you.

My prayer is that, with the help of this book, each of your days will be filled with blessings, miracles, and joy.

— **Doreen Virtue**

1

ALL your tomorrows are well taken care of by us. Have faith, and trust that your needs will always be met, now and in the future.

CALLING upon us angels is a
powerful way to bring light
and love into any situation.

ANYONE can call upon us; you need not belong to a certain religion or "earn" the right to do so.

ANGELIC help is the
Divine right and priv-
ilege of everyone.

THINK of us as a 24-hour hotline that never has a busy signal and never puts you on hold.

YOU can call upon us by thinking the thought, *Angels, please help me!*; mentally or verbally telling your troubles to us; asking God to send more of us to you; visualizing us surrounding you or your loved ones; writing a letter to us; and using angel oracle cards.

IT is not so important *how* you contact us, but that you *do* contact us.

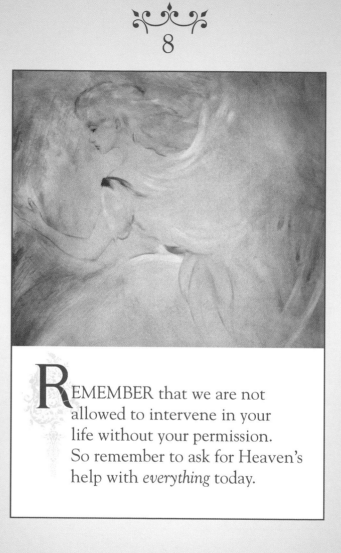

REMEMBER that we are not allowed to intervene in your life without your permission. So remember to ask for Heaven's help with *everything* today.

SINCE we are extensions and messengers of God, whether you ask us directly or send your request to the Creator, the results are the same.

THINK of us as Divine mail carriers, bringing messages of love and light from the Creator to the created.

WE angels illuminate your mind and heart with a big infusion of light. We help you see the Divine truth of situations through the fog of fearful illusion.

WE remind you that, despite all appearances to the contrary, everything really is okay in the end.

WE can help you heal *anything*—without exception.

YOU do not need to struggle with anything in life, including material objects or your finances.

WE assist you with your daily life so that you will be healthier and happier each day. This includes helping you get a good night's sleep.

YOU can ask us to come into your dreams and clear away emotional or physical distress. You may not recall the dream the next morning, but you will know that you were visited.

SOMETIMES your prayers are made on behalf of a loved one. These prayers are just as power-ful for another as they are for yourself—provided that the other person is willing to be healed.

CHILDREN are naturally attracted to working with us, and they find great comfort in calling upon Heaven for help.

WHEN you invoke us angels for others, you may often receive signs as validation that we have appeared. This confirmation may come as a physical sign, an inner knowing, a feeling, or a healing.

INVOKING us is one of the most powerful and profoundly healing activities you can perform in the face of seeming illness or injury.

E VEN if you are unsure or dis-
believing, the act of calling
upon us has immediate benefits
for you if you are ill—as well as
for your loved ones.

SPREAD your wings and fly
in complete confidence,
Earth angel!

YOU are supported with the same energy that holds the planets in the sky. If God can support the huge planet Jupiter, He can certainly do the same for you.

HOLD only thoughts of love and success, and you are assured of only attracting love and success into your life.

YOU are loved, guided, and protected by us, your guardian angels, now and always.

K NOW that we see your true talent, beauty, and wisdom.

W E, your guardian angels, know every aspect of your Divine life purpose and will give you guidance and answers if you will simply ask.

INVITE us to come into your dreams to answer your questions and concerns. While asleep, your mind is more open to Divine guidance.

WE will do whatever is necessary to bring you peace.

NEVER worry that you are bothering us with your requests. We are here to help you with *anything* that brings you peace.

WE angels watch over skeptics and believers alike.

WE look past surface personality characteristics and see the beautiful, pure light of God within each person. Today, try to see yourself and others as we do . . . with love.

33

OPEN your heart to our love. It is profound, sweet, warm, and healing.

FOLLOW the wisdom of the inner voice that guides you with love and light.

EVEN a rhetorical cry for help, such as, *If anyone can hear me, please help!* is enough to invoke our assistance.

As you release any fears that block you from receiving and recognizing messages from us, you become more aware of the presence of love in your life.

WE angels are with you as
a gift from the Creator;
and our aim is to establish
peace on Earth, one person
at a time.

YOU who seek answers will find them, as you consult us while reading our words.

WE are your angels, and we shall love you throughout eternity.

YOUR love *is* happiness, *is* peace, *is* immortality, and *is* abundantly cared for.

YOU are the product of Divine creation, and as such, you are already completely formed in all ways.

DIVINE love always has been, and always will be, the answer that you seek.

43

LEARN and grow gently, by "unlearning" pain and remembering love, and you shall unravel the entanglements that once snared you.

44

LET not one more moment slip by without an awareness of the pulsating love that beats steadily within you like a drum's rhythms, perfectly synchronized with God's outpouring of joy.

REMEMBER to bring a sense of the sacred into your romantic love relationship, and to seek for safety and shelter together in the only place that it can be found: in God within.

YOU are home, you are safe, and you are loved, now and always.

THE ego urges you to accomplish, while the soul merely asks you to enjoy the process.

YOUR loved ones are never out of reach—not now or ever—for souls are constantly in communication with one another, especially when familial love is involved.

YOUR soul, incapable of lies or capriciousness, knows that all your loved ones—on the Earth plane and beyond—are at this very moment enshrouded in God's ecstatic joy.

TRUE joining with your loved ones comes from connecting with them in the inner glow of God's eternal joy.

WHEN you transmit joy to your loved ones, there is a bond so deep that it runs without words.

JOY is all there is. The rest is a preoccupation of the ego, unworthy of your holy mind.

EMOTIONAL healing does not mean dwelling upon the wound; it means looking at the world through unwounded eyes.

YOUR true and inner self is unscarred, unwounded, and fully confident in living a peaceful life so that all may benefit.

WHAT you set your heart upon
must come about.

WE are the angels who are among you night and day, and who steadfastly refuse to see you in any way except by the holy light that burns within you.

BELOVED Child of God,
you have done nothing wrong,
and we assure you that you are
wholly lovable—then, now,
and always.

MOVE on into eternity with a gladdened heart, knowing that your true Father and Mother in Heaven will love and comfort you always.

GIVE the situation to God and us angels, and know that we will effectively guide this challenge—and all involved.

YOU are given the power to heal, a power so lovely that if you cast your eyes before it, you would fall to your knees in awe of the Creator's great gift to you!

FORGIVE yourself, Darling Child of God, for your harsh judgments of your reality!

IN each situation, ask whether each thought, each word, and each deed creates a greater or a lesser awareness of love.

THERE is nothing to fear or worry about, Dear One. You and your loved ones are cradled and protected by the strength and love of God.

IN truth, love is all there is. Everything else is just an illusion and therefore unworthy of your time, energy, or attention.

YOU can fly as free as a bird, without constraint or time restrictions. You can achieve this right now!

THE only restriction is the limitation in your beliefs that prevents you from breaking free from self-made imprisonment.

YOU truly hold the key to your prison by imagining the cell door being opened wide.

As you open your prison doors widely, so do you allow others the escape they desire.

IN addition to showing gratitude to others, place emphasis on showing gratitude to yourself.

YOUR heart-center glows brightly with love as you praise it for its very existence.

PRAISE your inner glow so that its embers may burn even brighter.

GIVE thanks to God so that you may extend this love ever outward in a widening circle of gladness.

DO not see God as separated from your inner embers. Know that He created, and continues to stoke, this original flame.

YOUR light can never be extinguished. Your only task is to ensure that its glow burns ever more brightly, allowing it to shine for all to see.

ALWAYS remember that God's Divine light burns within you, now and forever.

YOUR powerful heart-center is God's gift during your earthly journey—it guides you, manifests for you, and clears you of any wreckage along the way.

LIGHTEN your heart by engaging
in enjoyable activities: Sing,
dance, watch the sunset, take
a nap, or hug someone with
exuberance.

IN God's eyes, you and your fellow human beings are the most beautiful creatures in the Universe.

WE look past your earthly mistakes and see the eternal flame of Divine love within you.

SAY to yourself,
"I am love. I am light."
See it, and know it to be true.

EVERYTHING is already healed, except in the dream of illness. Let the illusion go, in exchange for peace.

SIMPLY see the situation, no matter its topic or appearance, as already resolved. Give thanks that it is so.

EVEN an ounce of belief will go far along the pathway to revealing the healed under-pinnings of every seeming problem.

HOLD the truth in consciousness
that sickness cannot exist in the
face of love, and you will reveal
the greatest reality of them all.

Healing, when properly understood, merely means casting a firm decision in the direction of your Higher Self's priorities.

YOUR access to health is eternally available, and you need merely claim this because you desire more available time and energy for your holy purpose.

Y OUR clear and unwavering decision for health cannot be obstructed, Holy Child of God.

YOUR unquestionable power rests upon your decision, your intention, and your commitment.

THERE is no force opposed to your own. In this, your will and God's will co-exist in perfect harmony.

BECOMING natural means
that you trust and follow the
guidance of your heart.

I F there is something that you desire, you have the means to attain it.

YOU only need to be clear about what it is that you want, pray for guidance, and then motivate yourself to take the necessary steps that are guided.

THE power is yours at any given moment.

MYRIAD solutions await your beck and call, if only you will set your mind on the dial of "solutions" instead of "problems."

95

GOD cannot thrust solutions onto you, but He does await your prayers for guidance to help you reach your own happy endings.

YOU have much to offer the world, Dear One! You are multitalented beyond your scope of understanding.

YOU have the power, with your focused intention, to create a career that is rooted in your life's purpose.

OUR prayer is that you will call upon us for guidance, and that you will surely follow it as it is given.

EVERY moment of your life is a chance to serve, and thus, is an opportunity to be joyful.

100

ONE of the reasons why we
angels are so joyful is that
we are continuously focused
upon giving service.

GIVING from a place of abundance, where you know that you have much to give, brings joy to all.

SEARCH the horizon for opportunities to serve and they present themselves readily to you.

YOU have angels assisting you in your healing, teaching, and service work, so do not hesitate to call upon us to support you.

YOUR intentions create your experiences, so hold intentions to only see, feel, and experience your highest good.

BE open to receiving the good
that comes to you each day.

THROUGH gracious receiving, you know that you are amply blessed.

107

WHEN you place your faith in the Creator within and above as the Source for which you have been waiting, you can move ahead easily.

108

THERE is nothing and no
one preventing you from
enjoying your life purpose.

YOU are an entirely free agent,
no matter what appearances
may seem to prevail.

AT every moment, there is a
person or situation who could
benefit from your application of
Divine light, love, and vision.

＊＊＊＊＊
111

ALWAYS remember that you are
the director of the movie script
in which you find yourself.

A positive intention will bring
you your desired outcomes,
and a pessimistic intention
will always block you.

WHAT you set your sights upon, with clear intention, is what you steer toward. It is what you draw into your life.

GOD'S will, which resides within you always, directs you toward happiness by reminding you that you are already immersed in joy.

THE pleasure you seek is attained the instant you allow yourself to enjoy the gift that is already given to you.

WHEN you are willing to consult Divine guidance about *everything*, you are free to let go and enjoy living.

NO matter what the material or situational intention, approach it with the desire for joy.

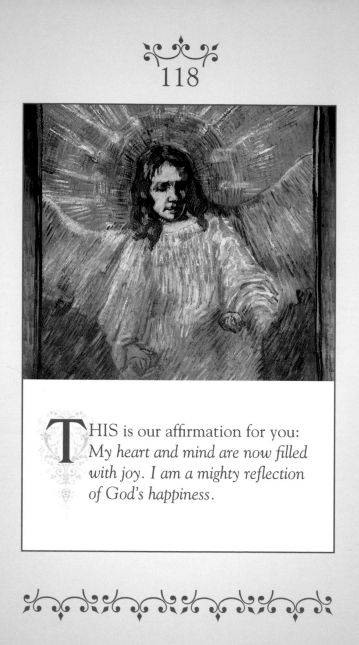

THIS is our affirmation for you: *My heart and mind are now filled with joy. I am a mighty reflection of God's happiness.*

JOY keeps you strong and provides you access to creative wisdom.

IT is possible to find joy, no matter what your outward circumstances appear to be.

REMEMBER that you are a child of God, blessed with peace and prosperity.

USE music to elevate your frequency as often as possible, since it bathes you in shimmering light that deflects negativity.

SIMPLY call upon us, and we will guide you without hesitation, without interference or control, and always with love.

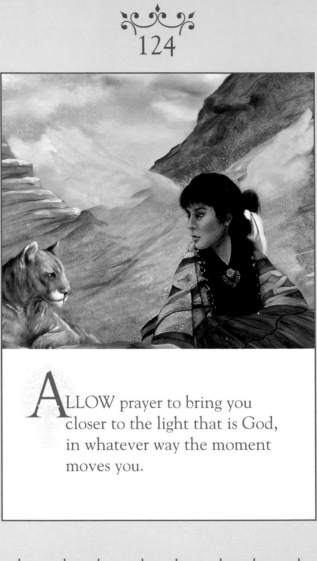

ALLOW prayer to bring you
closer to the light that is God,
in whatever way the moment
moves you.

B E in the moment with your prayer, and accept whatever thoughts or feelings present themselves to you.

EACH moment spent in prayer is like a coin put into a bank account.

THROUGHOUT the day, reach up and inwardly connect with us through thoughtful prayer and meditation.

SIMPLY cast your cares unto us, and let us cart them away as a janitor would carry away your garbage.

YOU have no worries that you cannot thrust into our loving and awaiting arms, Dear One. Give them all away!

PRAYER simply means "reconnection," and reconnection with the Divine is your lifeline to endless inspiration and vitality.

Y OU can engage in prayer during any moment of the day simply by holding in mind the intention to call home to Heaven.

HOLD the thought that you would like God's loving assistance, and it is done.

133

BE assured that we are always
available to assist you, and
know that your prayers will
never be denied.

ADMIRE everyone's beauty freely,
and drink in the perfume of Spirit
that is all around you.

USE your spiritual gifts to shower the world with Divine light.

YOU have the power to create or eliminate stress, debt, and pain. Today, choose peace.

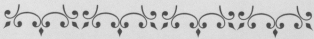

YOUR soul needs no progress, for it has never left God's side, and has never forgotten its holy self and wondrous gifts!

YOU are supplied, you are home, and you are safe— now and forever.

ONLY through casting your inevitable cares and worries to the true source of love—God— can a partnership remain on the highest plane possible.

I F you notice seven instances
where you see love being
expressed during the day,
depression can be eradicated.

FORGET not your Heavenly Creator, Who steadily resides within you now.

YOU, who have the power of all of Heaven's spheres within you, need never believe that you are a victim of outside circumstances.

143

YOU are as holy as any of Heaven's creations.

YOU are a shining example of God's handiwork, encapsulated in a being so lovely that all of Heaven breathes deeply at the sight of you.

DO you not realize that we angels love you eternally; and that we work tirelessly to bring you through periods of restlessness, sorrow, and peril into the light of joy?

EVERYTHING is built in
your favor, Dear One, and
we await your decision to
stand in the light of this joy.

EACH partnership comes to you for a specific reason and purpose.

148

WHEN you meet your soul mate, do not seek to capture this person, but enjoy and delight in his or her Heavenly gifts.

WE angels kiss you with gratitude, as God's Divine grace and love shines upon you.

WHEREVER you find stress, you will also find feelings of victimhood. Your God-given power ensures that you can never be a victim, except in belief.

ALL stress is self-imposed, since
all stress-inducing situations are
elected by your own free will.
You also have the free will to
reduce or eliminate stress.

PAIN is a time deceiver, covering the holes in your schedule that ache to be devoted toward your life's purpose.

WHEN you feel stress, call upon us angels, and allow us to open the doors of self-made prisons that you have barred yourself behind.

ALLOW us to fan the flames of your Divine light so that you can step up to your life's purpose without hesitation, delay, or compromise.

YOU are born to take this power out into the world and experience it as the life-changing force that brings great joy to many.

YOU are meant to move forward in large, sweeping motions; and subtle, soft breaths.

YOUR soul knows that uncovering its natural happiness lies in extending its joy outward, like a spring bubbling forth with its precious gift of water.

YOU have always been able to cope with each situation that has presented itself to you. This is as true of your future as it is of your past.

159

YOU must trust that you will be ready for whatever comes along. You will not perish, be abandoned, or starve in any way. All will be provided for you on your path.

WHENEVER you extend pity, you reinforce the suffering. But whenever you extend compassion and love, you end the suffering.

THE Creator is a mighty and powerful essence of all-encompassing love. This love is so bright that it deflects all darkness.

DARKNESS is simply unable to penetrate the intensely bright glare of the One. It is literally cast away by the beaming brightness.

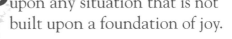

BE as the Creator, and shine light upon any situation that is not built upon a foundation of joy.

YOU act as the earthly angel who forms a bridge of light, allowing others to come home.

YOU *do* have great love within you at this very moment.

MIRACLES rush toward those who love so completely; and if you accept love through a human relationship, it shall be yours indeed.

THROUGH this stillness, you hear our words carried upon the silence of your breath.

WE do see your outcome with each choice that you make, and we seek only to encourage you whenever possible to make the choice for happiness in all ways.

SIT back and quietly reach an
awareness of this great light
that is within and around you
right now.

BRING forth miracles, Beloved One, by showering light from your heart, your mind, and your head, blanketing all the many dimensions with this gift of illumination.

YOU need to awaken your sleeping brothers and sisters by shining your light at all times.

PEACE is stimulating and quite exciting when truly experienced and understood.

PEACEFULNESS means having the courage to always love, without fear of repercussions.

NOTHING can be disordered
in this Universe, but you can
think it so.

THE more you allow us to help you, the more you will be able to help others. And the more you allow yourself to receive our gifts, the more you will have available to give to others.

OUR love for you is constantly outpouring from our hearts to yours—and we mean this for every human who could possibly hear these words.

WE are constantly pouring love on situations, in the manner of firefighters who are busily extinguishing the bitterly raging blaze.

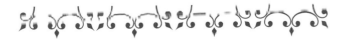

ARCHANGEL Gabriel is the ever-present helper, assisting those with brilliant and creative minds, and channeling this creativity into helpfulness upon the planet.

WHEN you take a clear-eyed and honest inventory of your present-day situation, you know that you are imbued with the power to address all concerns. Fearlessly look at your life today.

WE angels will lead you past the darkness and show you to the light that dwells within you.

WE will hold you with loving firmness so that you shall not be afraid when you gaze upon your Holy Self.

THE truth shall cast away all your fears, as we gently guide you to look within with loving honesty.

WE are here in stewardship of this great planet, and we do everything we can to assist you.

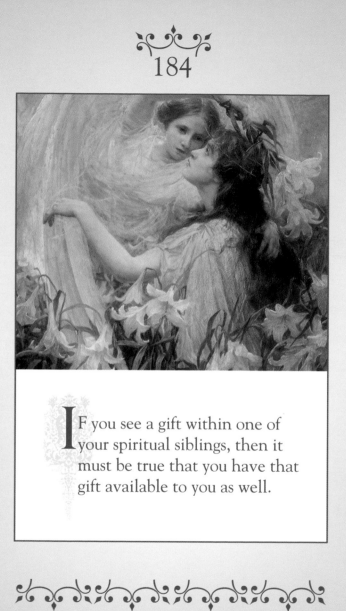

IF you see a gift within one of your spiritual siblings, then it must be true that you have that gift available to you as well.

185

BE grateful for those who have opened the door before you, for they have shown you new possibilities.

SEEING sparkles or flashes
of light indicates that we
are nearby.

THE more you can accept your true heritage as celestial, as a being spawned by great love, the more willing you will be to accept the benefits that accompany all Children of Love.

188

YOUR presence in the world makes all beings glad, and we seek to do the same unto you!

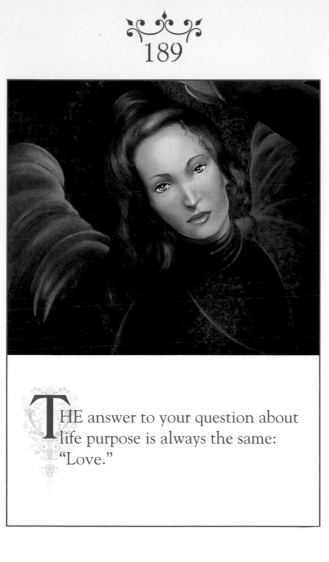

THE answer to your question about life purpose is always the same: "Love."

USE each moment to make another's eyes sparkle and to warm a heart.

USE your comforting power to reach out to those in need, and your able hands to relieve stress on Earth's Godly plains.

PUT into motion all of your good intentions today. Ask us to assist, and we will happily do so.

*B*E happy that you already *are* happy, and it is so.

194

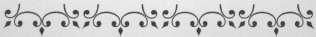

AN answered prayer does not always mean that your "wishes" come true, but it does mean that attention is given to you and the situation without delay.

THERE can be no other possible outcome than happiness and love, because nothing else *is* possible.

IF you can trust God and His handiworkers to give you comfort, aid, and assurance, you will be opening your arms to receiving these gifts.

DO not chase anything, but instead, ask and be open to receiving.

GOD wills more good for you than you do yourself!

WHEN you inflict conditions upon your happiness, you place that joy in a future tense.

THERE is not one iota in God's consciousness that would test you or give you pain. God wills only love, joy, and peace for you in all ways.

ALLOW us to bestow upon you the tools that are needed so that you, too, may shower the world with your gifts.

INFINITE Wisdom has many courses to choose from, and you would not want to steer it toward one of less satisfaction through an insistence on one certain way.

WORKING in conjunction with Heavenly guides, your changes will come about in a monumental way.

AS you make your changes, they
will go as quickly as you feel
comfortable.

205

SHOULD you desire an instant change, that is certainly available to you, as your heart desires.

SEE the inner joy within everyone, regardless of the surface conditions that appear.

As you see the holiness within others, you more readily see this Divinity within your own self.

*K*NOW that you are God's lovely child!

WITH trust, the rest falls easily into place.

BEGIN sharing with your partner the contents of your heart: your dreams and desires.

BE very honest with yourself about all the aspects of this situation that you are considering.

CONCENTRATE on giving service in a way that brings you great pleasure and enjoyment. Make your only focus "How may I serve?" and everything will be given unto you.

KNOW that we are with you in your current job, and in any future endeavors you might pursue.

YOUR soul will keep you safe and give you the clear and loving guidance you seek.

BE not afraid of your own
greatness, but allow us to
mirror it for you during our
communications.

As you witness our greatness visually, and with naked ears fully opened to love's voice, there you will witness your own Divinity.

AN emotional or physical block is not a reality unless you focus upon it in a constant state of awareness.

EACH relationship has, at
its heart, a holy purpose.

WE angels could never cease to love you, not now or ever.

UPLIFT the people in your life
by surrounding them in an aura
of the whitest light.

221

KNOW that your loved ones are being taken care of—whether they are in the physical plane or among us in the spirit world.

WE shall not let go of your loved ones, nor of you.

NO matter what physical actions a human may make, our love goes on without condition or judgment.

BE gentle with yourselves,
Dearest Ones, and know that
you live close to God's heart.

YOU, who have such power
that it is unequaled by any other,
could no more be powerless than
could God.

W E, who are assigned to watch over your care, come directly from the same Great Mind that is within each one of you.

THE bliss of the Creator forever permeates all of creation, and it is only in the forgetting that misery exists.

YOU are already in the midst of God's blissful reality, and you need not seek it a moment longer.

W E help you to remember your Divine nature, to be loving and kind, to discover and polish your talents for the betterment of the world, and to keep yourself from harm's way before your time.

230

WE are with you to enact
God's plan of peace.

WE angels help you be more peaceful, because one person at a time, a world of peaceful people equals a peaceful world.

YOU aren't wasting our time if you ask for "small" favors. After all, there are unlimited numbers of us, with unlimited amounts of time.

WHILE it is true that challenges do make you grow, peace leads to even bigger growth spurts.

234

BY being a reflection of peacefulness, you are a shining example of God's love.

WE, your guardian angels, are personally assigned to you for your entire life. You are never alone.

EACH of you—regardless of faith, character, or lifestyle— has at least two guardian angels. Whether you choose to listen to us, though, is an entirely different matter.

EVERYONE has an equal
ability to communicate with
us, because everyone is equally
"gifted" spiritually.

THE more you can relax, the more easily you will be able to consciously commune with us.

CHILDREN do not care whether they are imagining their angel visions; they simply enjoy and accept them. As a result, little ones easily see and hear us, their guardian angels.

ALLOW no fear to "inter-fear" with your domain of happiness, for that is God's Kingdom of great blessings.

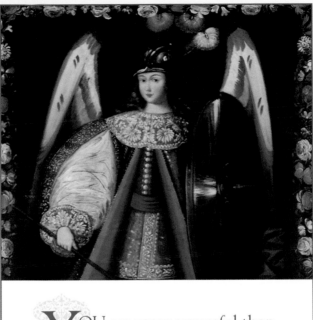

YOU are more powerful than any fearful force. Your Divine willingness can out-will any darkness that the world has ever seen.

TRUE angelic experiences
feel warm, safe, loving, and
comfortable.

WE speak to you in response to your queries. So, you can kick-start a conversation simply by directing a question to us.

IS there a question that you have, or some area of your life in which you desire guidance? Take a moment right now and mentally ask us your question.

EVEN if you cannot hear us
answering you right now, be
assured that we can definitely
hear you!

WE orbit around you much like you see the stars in the sky hovering around nearby planets.

NO matter what, you can always count on our unconditional and continuous love.

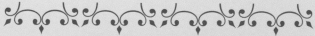

LOOKING up at the sky and noticing a cloud in the shape of an angel is another way we let you know that we are with you.

249

FINDING a feather, a coin, a stopped clock, moved objects in your home, lights flickering, the television set turning off or on independently, or other visual oddities let you know that one of us is saying, "Hello, I am here."

SEEING a mental movie that provides you with true information about a person or situation, or that gives you guidance about your life purpose or making changes, is a sign of being in our presence.

251

ANYONE can receive messages
from us. In fact, you are receiving messages from your angels
. . . *right now!*

GUILT lowers your physical and spiritual energy, while joy elevates you and allows you to fly. Give us your guilt and we will transmute it into joy.

IF you would feel more peaceful if you received financial assistance, entered into a great love relationship, or secured a better job, then the angels are helping you with a sacred mission indeed.

THERE is no request that is too trivial or too monumental for us.

KNOW that you deserve love, attention, and miraculous blessings from us. We love you unconditionally, no matter what mistakes you may have made in your life.

ALLOW yourself to be open to our messages.

OUR messages will always help you feel safer and happier, and will make every aspect of your life more meaningful.

YOU can call more of us to your side (or to the side of your loved ones) simply by holding the thought that you would like to be in contact with additional angels.

WE want to help you and give you messages, if only you will let us.

THE more that you allow Heaven to help you, the more resources you will have to give back to the world.

WHEN you develop the habit of getting us involved in every area of your life, you will function like a member of a successful sports team.

YOU learn through peace, and more important, you can better teach your children and others when you are in a state of joyful relaxation.

GOD certainly does not want you to endure pain, any more than you want your own loved ones to do so.

BY tuning in to our messages, you can help create a peaceful world . . . one person at a time.

YOU are indeed an Earth angel sent here by God to perform miraculous deeds of love and sharing.

YOU are beloved and loving, and we Heavenly angels are here to support and guide you.

WE angels will help you purify your body, mind, and spirit of any lower energies that could rob you of the health and happiness that is your Divine birthright.

YOU are never alone, and we accompany you constantly, even when you are unaware of our presence.

WE want to interact with you more frequently. We would love to be fully involved with every aspect of your life, yet we cannot help you unless you specifically ask.

LIKE many parts of life that are good for you, such as meditation and exercise, you benefit by making angelic communication a regular part of your life.

SURROUND yourself with
reminders such as angel statues
and posters so that you will
not forget to call upon us, your
Heavenly friends, for help and
assistance.

YOU need not wait until a crisis or some other dilemma has hit before asking us for help. In fact, it is a good idea to work with us in any trying situation before it gets to the boiling point.

THERE are no limits to what we can do in your life. We are very, very powerful beings.

ONCE you ask us into your life, get ready, because your journey will change in miraculous ways.

IF you do not yet fully believe in us, you will know that we are real after asking for and receiving our help two or three times.

THE angelic kingdom loves you, and we see you as you truly are on the inside.

WE perceive you as an innocent and perfect Child of God.

WE know that you have made occasional mistakes, yet we overlook your errors and see the love and good intentions within your heart.

SEE yourself and others through the eyes of an angel and you will see a beautiful world that is light, bright, and hopeful.

YOU *are* an angel, and you are a blessing to the world.

281

INSTEAD of trying to control or fix negative situations on a human level, we work with you from the spiritual plane.

WE angels continuously remind you that you have all the power you need, right inside yourself.

WE are kin, in that we are all creations of the same all-powerful, all-loving Maker.

PENETRATING our loving guardianship is impossible for any negative forces to do.

285

IF you are in an unfamiliar environment, or anywhere you feel unsafe or dishonored, call upon us for protection and we will help you instantly and without question.

NO matter what you need help with, no matter what you believe your blocks or limitations to be, we have a solution waiting for you right now. Just ask us.

WE really want to help you regain the joy of loving God! We ask for your willingness to hand the entire situation over to us for repair.

TELL us about all your cares, upsets, and fears. Don't worry—there are no negative repercussions for honesty, especially since we are already aware of everything you are going to say.

WE remind you that every negative feeling you hold toward another has a boomerang effect. It is impossible to judge or blame someone else and not feel emotional pain.

290

BEFORE doing anything, ask your Higher Self, God, and us angels to guide you. In this way, you are assured of continually floating in a sea of miracles that will astound you with their beauty.

GIVE your motivations to God and ask that they be purified. Say, "I give You my motivations and ask for Your help in purifying them so that all my motives are aligned with truth and love."

THERE are no neutral thoughts, nor moments in the day, when your thoughts do not create thought-forms and their causative effects.

293

If you need more faith or belief, ask us to help you and you will feel a shift very soon.

IF you feel undeserving of Divine intervention, simply ask for our assistance in bolstering your faith.

IF you are accustomed to taking care of everyone else, you will need to be patient with yourself while you develop the new habit of accepting help from us.

WE want to communicate clearly with you. We have so much to give you!

WE are with you wherever you go, so we are not concerned about *where* you choose to talk to us.

If asking for, and accepting, Divine assistance feels unnatural to you, ask us to help you change this tendency.

WE can heal away low self-esteem and any personality characteristic that gives you pain.

KNOW that you are worthy of help from us! You are a precious and holy Child of God, and you deserve all that is good.

ASK us to tell you our names. Then be very still and listen. The answer may come intuitively, and you may get a feeling about the name or hear an inner voice say it.

WE angels are not that difficult to hear if you listen for us with an open heart. Most of the time we are closer to you than you can imagine.

303

OUR angelic voices are consistently loving and supportive, even when we warn you of impending danger or wrong turns.

NOT everyone "hears" our voices as audible sounds. Many people receive Divine messages through nonverbal means, such as visions, feelings, or a knowingness.

305

IT is easier to hear us when you are alone, especially when you are in a natural setting.

YOUR guardian angel continuously talks to you, and gently offers advice and guidance.

WE hear the prayers of your heart, and if you mentally cry for help, we will flock to your side.

PARENTS can ask for angelic babysitters to guide and protect your children throughout the day.

WE want to surround you, and we truly wish to give you help. Your joy brings *us* enormous happiness.

To us angels, no job is big or small—they are all expressions of the love we have for you.

311

IF your request for angelic
assistance is sincere, we
appear in response to your
call, often before you have
finished invoking us!

GOD'S thoughts of love created us. Since the Creator's loving thoughts are unlimited, there is an unlimited number of us angels.

WE are here to help you, especially when your intent is to bring joy and healing to the world.

ASK for as many of us as you
want to be a part of your life.

ASK for us to protect your loved ones, your home, your vehicle, and your business.

WE receive great joy when we help you, and we only ask that you occasionally remember to say "Thank you" in gratitude for our help. Even then, this gratitude is more to benefit yourself than us.

SINCE joy is our primary
emotion, you are sure to
feel immense pleasure as
you consciously connect
with us angels.

DIVINE guidance is not limited to profound revelations. Messages from Heaven are mostly profound in their simplicity.

ORDINARY events become a pleasure instead of a chore as you become aware of the invisible team that surrounds you.

WE love to help you while
you are driving, dressing,
dining, dancing—that is,
while engaging in virtually all
human activities from A to Z.

WE speak to each of you continuously, and you all have the equal potential to receive and understand our words.

322

HEAVEN does not just work miracles to pull you out of messes. We help you with everyday, ordinary situations as well.

WE give you practical, prescriptive advice about how to solve your dilemmas, remedy your hurts, and resolve your challenges.

WE, your guardian angels, know you better than you know yourself, since we were assigned to you at birth and have watched you grow and evolve.

WE watch over you personally,
and we always know what is
best for you.

WE are happy to offer you our solutions, as your happiness makes us happy and is a fulfillment of God's will.

GOD loves all of His children equally, and sends us angels and our messages to help all of you who ask.

DO not be afraid to be powerful! Ask us to release you from any such fear.

329

WHEN you allow God to support you, you are in a better position to help other people.

A LOT of times we ask you to walk in faith when following our guidance. The outcome will always be filled with blessings, even if you do not know exactly what will happen.

YOU are frequently called upon to act as Earth angels in response to another's prayers.

EVERY time you smile
and feel happy, you are
fulfilling God's will.

333

WE can guide you to see the bright side of situations, to forgive, and to laugh.

SOMETIMES you needlessly worry about your future, not realizing, as we like to put it, that "you are the master of your day."

WE want to remind you that watches and clocks are machines, and that it is insane for a living being to compete with a mechanical device.

INSTEAD of fearing dark circumstances, know that you are eternally safe and protected.

YOU are surrounded by us right now; and we have so much love, wisdom, guidance, playful companionship, and healing energy to give you!

WE are with you continuously, ready to guide and help you whenever you ask.

ASK that we lovingly surround and protect your loved ones, your home, and your business.

NEVER worry about calling upon us because you fear that your need is not "big enough" or that one of us might be busy. We want to help you with everything, large or small.

341

YOUR call for help is sweet music to our ears.

YOU do not need to say a formal invitation or invocation ritual, and you do not even need to verbalize your call. Just the thought, *Angels!* is enough.

WE, your guardian angels and other members of the angelic realm, are happy to help release you from the negative effects of fearful thinking.

D ESPITE *anything* you have ever said, thought, or done, we love you unconditionally.

ASK for as many of us as you
like to be with you; there is
no shortage!

THE advantage of having additional angels is that you have an extra cushion of love energy around you, making you less vulnerable to problems and trouble.

SURRENDER and release
to us whatever is worrying
or bothering you, and we
will take it to the Light for
healing and transmutation.

BE open to receiving all the gifts and blessings that we are giving you today. These gifts often come to you as small miracles.

OY is the highest and most powerful emotion, and guilt is the lowest. Give any guilt to us so that we can turn it into joy!

WHAT are your heart's dreams and desires? Admit them to yourself and to us right now, and ask us to help you turn your dreams into reality.

YOU can heal arguments and misunderstandings by writing a letter to another person's guardian angels and asking them to bring peace to your relationship.

IF you think an unloving thought or one devoid of love—such as envy, worry, or resentment—you feel pain. Ask us to help you hold only loving thoughts.

WE respect you enormously, and we will never do anything to frighten you. If we know that it would scare you to see us, we will make sure that you do not do so until you are ready.

*E*VERYONE—no matter what their spiritual, religious, or educational background—can receive clear communications from the Divine spiritual realm.

355

HEAVEN gives you trustworthy answers to your deepest, most personal, and pressing questions.

YOU are God's greatest triumph, and as you revel in your recovered awareness of this simple fact, allow us to slip off all layers of painful soot collected through your travels.

WHEN you get in the habit of having continual conversations with us, your every action and thought is guided with powerful harmony.

Whenever you struggle, you put earplugs into your spiritual communication link with Heaven. You must relax and let go in order to hear us better.

359

As a child, you were aware of your contact with God and us angels. You can always reopen your connection with Heaven the moment you let go of your fears. Ask us to help with this "releasement."

SINCE we angels are a gift from the Creator, you are showing gratitude to God by enjoying this gift.

CHILDREN easily hear the voices of Heaven because they accept without question. Can you practice this open-mindedness, and know that Divine communication is as natural for you as it is for a child?

ALWAYS, Heaven reminds you to make choices based on love and not fear.

WE lovingly and gracefully guide you to a career that excites your passion and serves a purposeful function in the world, while also providing for all of your material needs.

NO question, challenge, or issue is too big or too trivial in God's eyes.

YOUR inner glow comes from the light of God, and your light can never be extinguished or soiled. You are eternally bright and beautiful!

About the Author

www.photographybycheryl.com

DOREEN VIRTUE, Ph.D.,** works with the angelic realm and is the best-selling author of the *Healing with the Angels* book and oracle cards and the *Messages from Your Angels* book and oracle cards, among many other products. Doreen lectures internationally, teaching audience members how to connect with their guardian angels. She has appeared on *Oprah*, CNN, and *Good Morning America*; and has been featured in numerous magazines and newspapers worldwide. Website: **www.AngelTherapy.com**

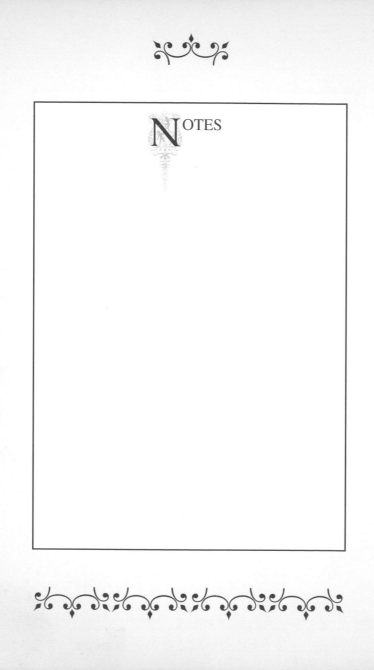

NOTES

NOTES

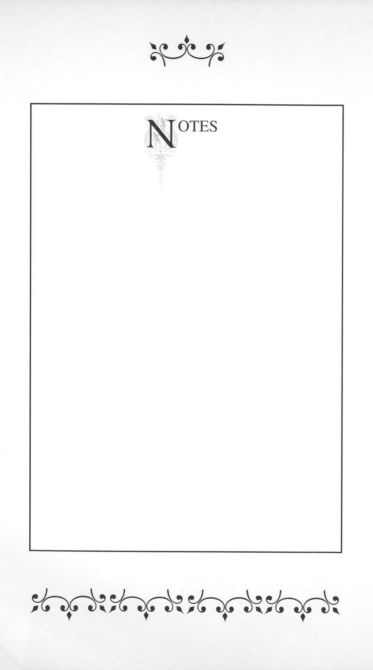

NOTES

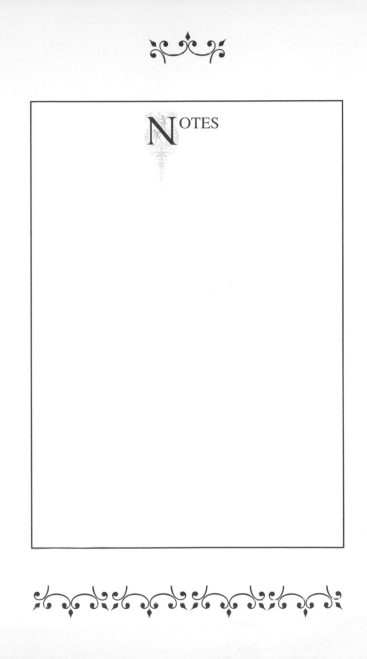

NOTES

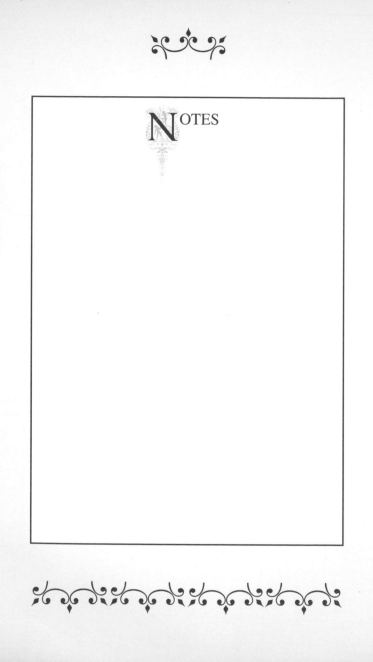

NOTES

NOTES

NOTES

Notes

Hay House Titles of Related Interest

The Invisible Force, by Dr. Wayne W. Dyer

Never Mind Success . . . Go for Greatness!
by Tavis Smiley

101 Ways to Jump-Start Your Intuition,
by John Holland

The Present Moment, by Louise L. Hay

Vitamins for the Soul, by Sonia Choquette

All of the above are available at your
local bookstore, or may be ordered by visiting:

Hay House USA: **www.hayhouse.com**®
Hay House Australia: **www.hayhouse.com.au**
Hay House UK: **www.hayhouse.co.uk**
Hay House South Africa: **www.hayhouse.co.za**
Hay House India: **www.hayhouse.co.in**